of their flippers, the baby turtles need to pop their heads above the water to take a breath.

With every eight revolutions

At dawn on the reef, diurnal fish (fish active during the day) wake and swish out of their beds under ledges or coral heads, then they swim off to get their gills cleaned and eat breakfast.

Nocturnal fish (fish active at night) swish into the same bed and fall asleep. This ritual is called "hot-bunking" because the fish's bed is always warm.

The Gulf Stream is from three to thirty miles off the east coast of Florida. In some places it is eighty miles wide, and it can be three thousand feet deep. It moves northward at 2.8 miles per hour.

Currents in the North Atlantic turn in a clockwise motion. In the South Atlantic, currents turn in a counterclockwise motion.

All sea turtles have a protective coating over their eyes to protect them from the stingers of their favorite food, jellyfish.

Scientists aren't sure why jellyfish stingers don't bother a turtle's mouth or stomach.

Scientists agree that overfishing in recent years has critically depleted the once-abundant sea life on the Grand Banks of Newfoundland. This giant underwater plateau is six hundred feet deep and four hundred miles wide.

The huge schools of fish that once thrived there are gone. If they are ever to make a comeback, then ships with enormous nets and longliners will have to be outlawed.

Scientists know through DNA tests that turtles from the beaches of Florida vacation on the coasts of France, Italy, Greece, and Spain.

Forty-two hundred cubic feet per second of water swirl through the equatorial zone, where the temperature on the surface of the ocean is so the hot, the water remains warm throughout the entire ninety-six-hundred-mile gyre.

Ocean Commotion

Ocean Commotion: Sea Turtles

Written and illustrated
by Janeen Mason

PELICAN PUBLISHING COMPANY

GRETNA 2006

To Women Supporting the Arts in Stuart, Florida, and to Sylvia Andrews, Jan Day, and Jeanette Wyneken, Ph.D. Without them this story would not be told. Thank you from the bottom of my turtle-loving toes. —J. M.

In Memory of Lundin Kudo

The word "Pelican" and the depiction of a pelican are trademarks of Pelican Publishing Company, Inc., and are registered in the U.S. Patent and Trademark Office.

Library of Congress Cataloging-in-Publication Data

Mason, Janeen I.
 Ocean commotion : sea turtles / written and illustrated by Janeen Mason.
   p. cm.
 ISBN-13: 978-1-58980-434-0 (hardcover : alk. paper)
 1. Loggerhead turtle—Juvenile literature. I. Title.
 QL666.C536M375 2006
 597.92'8—dc22

                    2006012494

Printed in Singapore

Published by Pelican Publishing Company, Inc.
1000 Burmaster Street, Gretna, Louisiana 70053

OCEAN COMMOTION: SEA TURTLES

Under the warm, silvery sand on a moonlit beach in Florida, a tiny turtle hatched from her soft white egg. All around her the jumble of other turtles shuffled and shifted. *Ouch!* Someone's flipper poked her in the eye. She felt the urge to crawl upward out of the crowded dark, but first she had to digest the last of her yolk.

Two more nights she lingered and when the sand near the surface was cool and damp against her beak, *wiggle, waggle, jiggle, squirm!* She set off a chain reaction. All the **hatchlings** began to fidget at once, and as the sand caved in around them, it created a turtle elevator they rode to the surface.

She was the first to **emerge.** The sand crust covering her eyes fell away when she blinked. She looked one way, then the other, and in that instant the dark shape of the shoreline was forever fixed in her memory. A hundred other turtles popped out all around her.

It was a **frenzy!** She dashed down the beach, away from the dunes and the trees. She toppled past a raccoon, skittered around a crab, and tumbled into the ocean. *I did it!* she thought.

In the confusion of the noise and bubbles of the
waves, she bobbled for a second, but when a big fish
splashed out of the water, her flippers spun like a
wind-up toy and she shot out of the shallows.

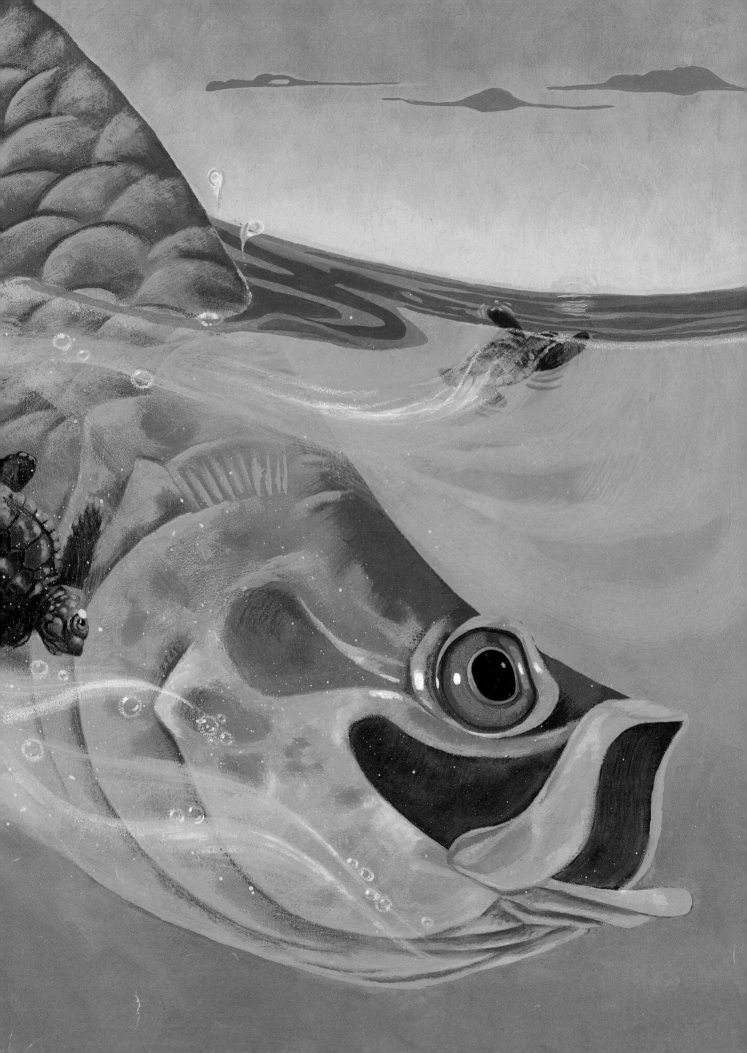

She saw fish on the reef below as they woke and stretched while others yawned and fell asleep. *Don't look up!* she thought. *Please don't look up.*

For three whole days, the tiny turtle swam. Every time she looked back, there were fewer hatchlings following her. On the third night, when she couldn't lift a flipper one more time, the **Gulf Stream** caught her in its **current.**

She rocked with the strong northward flow. A passing raft of **sargassum** tangled in her flippers. She wound its air sacs around her 2½-inch shell, fell sound asleep, and drifted through her exhausted dreams.

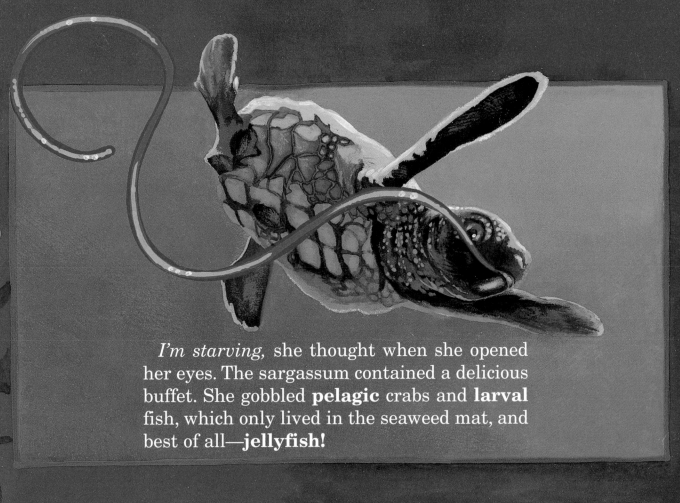

I'm starving, she thought when she opened her eyes. The sargassum contained a delicious buffet. She gobbled **pelagic** crabs and **larval** fish, which only lived in the seaweed mat, and best of all—**jellyfish!**

When sea birds circled above, she held her breath and wiggled deep into her floating home to hide.

When big fish hunted from below, she clambered to the top of the sargassum and kept an eyeball trained into the deep.

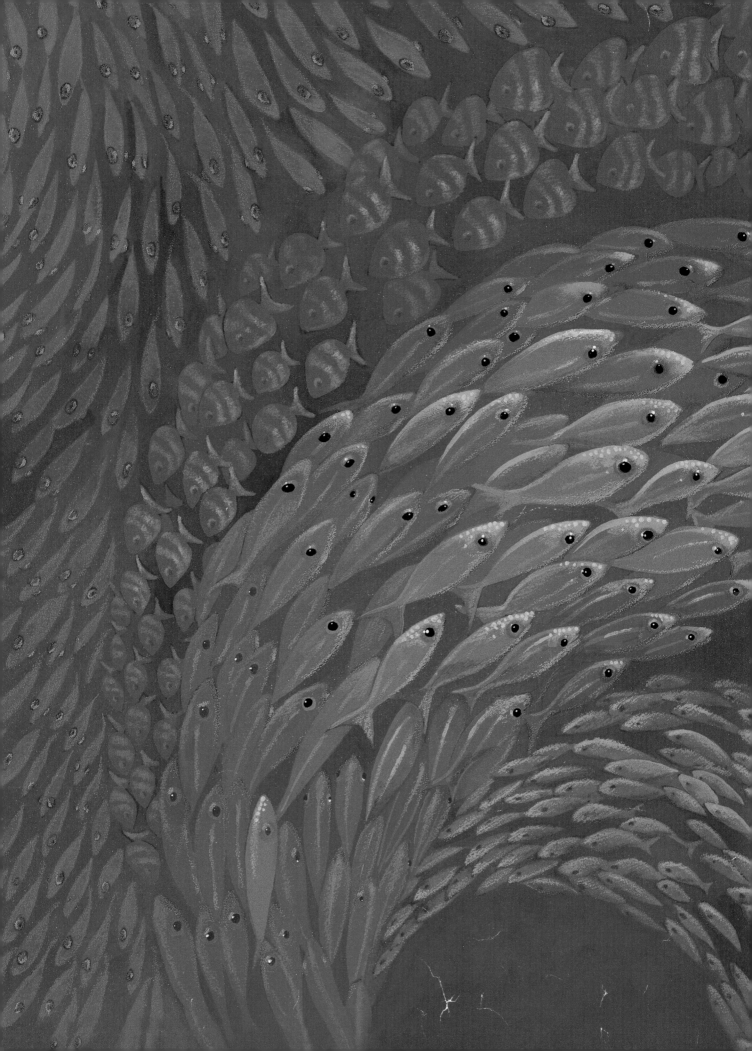

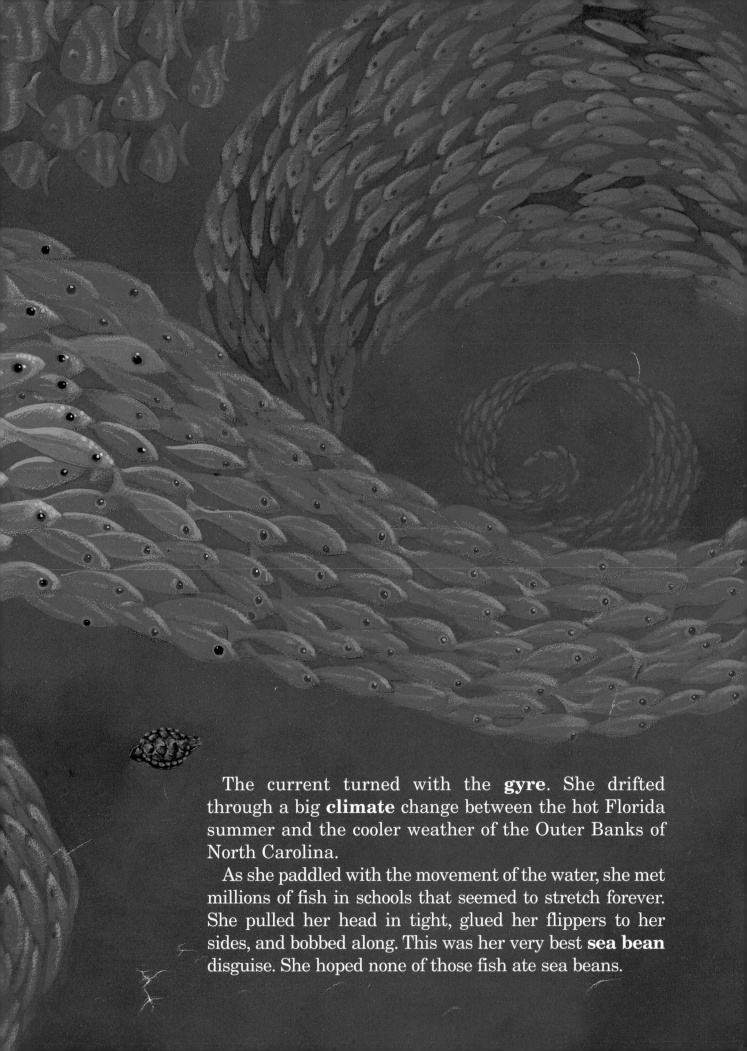

The current turned with the **gyre**. She drifted through a big **climate** change between the hot Florida summer and the cooler weather of the Outer Banks of North Carolina.

As she paddled with the movement of the water, she met millions of fish in schools that seemed to stretch forever. She pulled her head in tight, glued her flippers to her sides, and bobbed along. This was her very best **sea bean** disguise. She hoped none of those fish ate sea beans.

Land! All summer and fall she had drifted out of sight of land, and finally she reached the **Azores.** Little turtles arrived here daily from all over. The excited **juveniles** tumbled and twirled into the crowd like children on the first day of school.

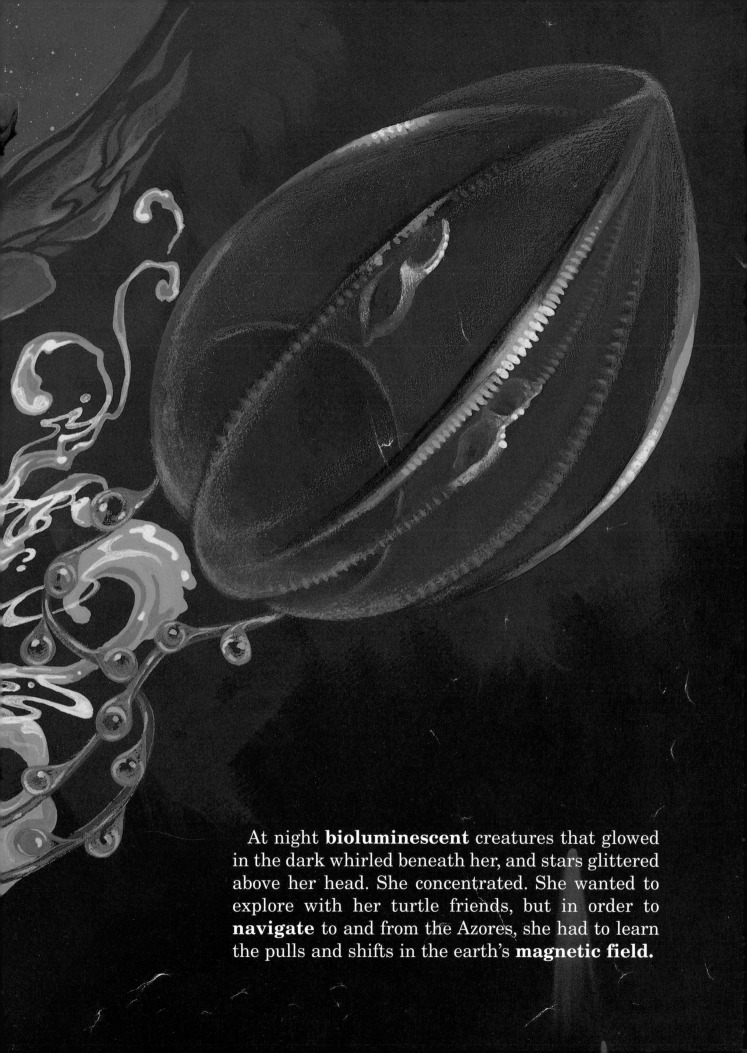

At night **bioluminescent** creatures that glowed in the dark whirled beneath her, and stars glittered above her head. She concentrated. She wanted to explore with her turtle friends, but in order to **navigate** to and from the Azores, she had to learn the pulls and shifts in the earth's **magnetic field.**

Each year more juveniles arrived in the waters near the islands, while the **adolescents,** or teenagers, departed forever on the outgoing current.

She grew bigger, faster, and smarter every season. One time she stretched out her beak to grab a shiny hook just as it was yanked away from her. She watched **longliners** haul out of the deep hundreds of creatures that had been caught by the hooks. *I'm never going to bite a hook,* she decided. *Never.*

Another time she was trapped with thousands and thousands of fish in a net. Luckily, the trapdoor of a **turtle excluder device** opened to let her escape. *I am never going near a net again. Never, ever,* she promised herself.

When her shell was fourteen inches long, she could take a big breath and dive really deep. She explored the ocean from the Grand Banks of Newfoundland to the Straits of Gibraltar.

At eighteen inches long, she could dive really deep and swim a long way. She swam over the canyons and mountains in the underwater range called the Mid-Atlantic Ridge.

At twenty inches long, she could dive really deep, swim a long way, and stay underwater for hours. She explored the Mediterranean Sea from one end to the other.

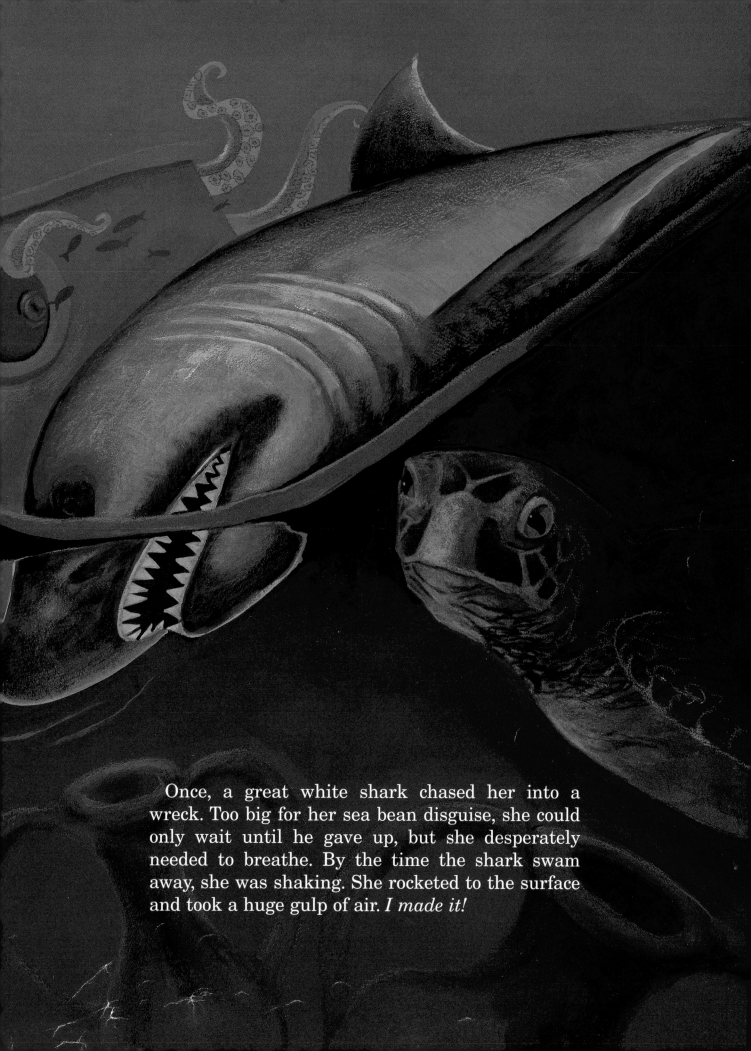

Once, a great white shark chased her into a wreck. Too big for her sea bean disguise, she could only wait until he gave up, but she desperately needed to breathe. By the time the shark swam away, she was shaking. She rocketed to the surface and took a huge gulp of air. *I made it!*

A springtime arrived when her shell measured twenty-five inches long. During her twelve years in the Azores, she had become an adolescent, and it was her turn to ride the outgoing current.

But she was scared. Her heart hammered in her ears. Then she remembered how far she drifted when she was just a tiny turtle, how she escaped when she was trapped in the net, and how she held her breath so long the day of the shark. *I can dive deep, swim a long way, and stay underwater for hours. I am big; I am fast; I am smart.* She paddled into the gyre.

She spent two days off the coast of Africa with a gentle blue whale and her calf.

Dolphins let her sleep in the middle of their pod over the **abyss.**

A manta ray jumped over her when she reached the Bahamas.

By summer she recognized her Florida shoreline.
Home! Waves pushed her closer to shore, her flippers
brushed the sandy bottom, but **instinct** didn't drive
her out of the sea just yet.

She explored every nook and **estuary** from Norfolk to San Salvador, and every year she visited her **natal** shore in Stuart to watch older females lumber out of the surf to nest.

It was her twenty-fifth year when she met a handsome young male off the island of Bimini. He could dive really deep, swim a long way, and stay underwater for hours. Together they rolled and played in the crystal blue current. She had found her turtle mate.

In the ocean she felt weightless, but when she
trundled up on shore for the first time, she discovered
every ounce of her three hundred pounds. She lugged
herself up the beach above the high **tide** line, where
she reached down and dug a deep hole. Saltwater
tears streamed down her cheeks and kept the sand
from scratching her eyes.

Big and fast and smart, she wished for each egg as
it dropped into the hole.

It seemed to take forever to **camouflage** her nest
with scoops of sand tossed this way and that.

She turned, groaned, and hauled herself back down to the sea. The water caught and lifted her, then she vanished under the surf. *I'll be back soon,* she thought. *I'll be back.*

Her deep turtle tracks, thirty-six inches wide, disappeared with each passing wave.

Glossary

abyss: deepest waters in the ocean

adolescent: the stage between juvenile and adult

Azores: a group of islands in the North Atlantic Ocean

bioluminescent: able to produce light from within

camouflage: a disguise so that something looks like its surroundings

climate: weather

current: movement of water in a certain direction

emerge: to come out of something

estuary: body of water open to the ocean but protected by land

frenzy: confusing motion

Gulf Stream: a warm ocean current that flows north from the Gulf of Mexico to Newfoundland

gyre: a giant current that circles around the North Atlantic Ocean

hatchling: a young animal freshly hatched from an egg

instinct: knowledge an animal is born with

jellyfish: sea creatures with soft bodies and long tentacles

juvenile: the stage between hatchling and adolescent

larval: describes animals in their undeveloped baby form

longliner: a fishing boat that uses a long fishing line with lots of hooks to catch many fish at a time

magnetic field: the earth's invisible lines of force

natal: at the time or place of birth

navigate: to find your way around

pelagic: describes creatures that live in the open ocean or near the ocean's surface

sargassum: floating ocean weed

sea bean: drifting ocean seed

tide: water level that rises and falls twice a day

turtle excluder device (TED): screen or rope mesh that acts as an escape hatch for turtles and sharks in shrimp trawling nets and fish nets

Note from the Author:

This book is about the life cycle of the loggerhead turtle, the most prevalent sea turtle species along Florida's nesting beaches. Other sea turtles in the world include the leatherback, Kemp's ridley, olive ridley, hawksbill, green, black, and flat back sea turtles. Every single one is endangered, and they need our help to survive and prosper. When you grow up, maybe you will invent better ways to keep endangered animals safe, or maybe you'll be a leader who outlaws longlining factory ships that harm fish and turtle populations in all of our oceans. I hope so!

For more information about sea turtles, please visit:
www.oceancommotionbooks.com
www.cccturtle.org
www.seaturtles.org
www.turtles.org
www.nmfs.noaa.gov/pr/species/turtles
http://accstr.ufl.edu
www.science.fau.edu/biology/faculty/JWyneken.htm

Loggerhead sea turtles live for seventy years. When a female reaches maturity, around twenty-five years old, she will lay up to six nests every year. Each nest contains one hundred eggs. In her lifetime a female will lay thirty-two thousand eggs. A mother loggerhead turtle can't stay to protect her eggs, so she has to be careful to dig her nest far above the high-tide line so that the baby turtles won't drown and deep enough that predators like raccoons and crabs can't find the nest. If all goes well, her hatchling turtles will emerge in two months.

Scientists are still studying how sea turtles navigate. Whether they find their way home by following the stars, by smell, or by sensing the magnetic lines in the earth remains a mystery. It is thought that only two turtles out of a nest of one hundred hatchlings survive and return to their original shores to reproduce. Once a male hatchling enters the water, he will never set flipper on land again. The temperature in the nest determines how many hatchlings will be boys or girls. If a nest is warmer, more girls will be hatched. Sea turtles don't feel gravity in the ocean, which is why they are so fast in the water but so slow on land. Loggerheads hatched on the east coast of the United States make only one complete revolution around the North Atlantic gyre in their lifetimes—as juveniles. Turtle hatchlings know that it is time to emerge from their nest when sand near the surface of the beach is cool. The cooler temperature tells the baby turtles that it is nighttime, when there are fewer predators waiting for them in the dark. It takes only ninety seconds for the hatchlings to dash from their nest to the sea. When hatchlings enter the sea, they have to swim at the surface because they are small and buoyant and can't yet dive.